"This series is a tremendous resource for those wanting to study and teach the Bible with an understanding of how the gospel is woven throughout Scripture. Here are gospel-minded pastors and scholars doing gospel business from all the Scriptures. This is a biblical and theological feast preparing God's people to apply the entire Bible to all of life with heart and mind wholly committed to Christ's priorities."

BRYAN CHAPELL, President Emeritus, Covenant Theological Seminary; Senior Pastor, Grace Presbyterian Church, Peoria, Illinois

"Mark Twain may have smiled when he wrote to a friend, 'I didn't have time to write you a short letter, so I wrote you a long letter.' But the truth of Twain's remark remains serious and universal, because well-reasoned, compact writing requires extra time and extra hard work. And this is what we have in the Crossway Bible study series *Knowing the Bible*. The skilled authors and notable editors provide the contours of each book of the Bible as well as the grand theological themes that bind them together as one Book. Here, in a 12-week format, are carefully wrought studies that will ignite the mind and the heart."

R. KENT HUGHES, Visiting Professor of Practical Theology, Westminster Theological Seminary

"*Knowing the Bible* brings together a gifted team of Bible teachers to produce a high-quality series of study guides. The coordinated focus of these materials is unique: biblical content, provocative questions, systematic theology, practical application, and the gospel story of God's grace presented all the way through Scripture."

PHILIP G. RYKEN, President, Wheaton College

"These *Knowing the Bible* volumes provide a significant and very welcome variation on the general run of inductive Bible studies. This series provides substantial instruction, as well as teaching through the very questions that are asked. *Knowing the Bible* then goes even further by showing how any given text links with the gospel, the whole Bible, and the formation of theology. I heartily endorse this orientation of individual books to the whole Bible and the gospel, and I applaud the demonstration that sound theology was not something invented later by Christians, but is right there in the pages of Scripture."

GRAEME L. GOLDSWORTHY, former lecturer, Moore Theological College; author, *According to Plan, Gospel and Kingdom, The Gospel in Revelation,* and *Gospel and Wisdom*

"What a gift to earnest, Bible-loving, Bible-searching believers! The organization and structure of the Bible study format presented through the *Knowing the Bible* series is so well conceived. Students of the Word are led to understand the content of passages through perceptive, guided questions, and they are given rich insights and application all along the way in the brief but illuminating sections that conclude each study. What potential growth in depth and breadth of understanding these studies offer! One can only pray that vast numbers of believers will discover more of God and the beauty of his Word through these rich studies."

BRUCE A. WARE, Professor of Christian Theology, The Southern Baptist Theological Seminary

KNOWING THE BIBLE

J. I. Packer, Theological Editor
Dane C. Ortlund, Series Editor
Lane T. Dennis, Executive Editor

•　　•　　•　　•　　•　　•

Genesis	Psalms	John	1–2 Thessalonians
Exodus	Proverbs	Acts	1–2 Timothy
Leviticus	Ecclesiastes	Romans	and Titus
Deuteronomy	Isaiah	1 Corinthians	Hebrews
Joshua	Jeremiah	2 Corinthians	James
Ruth and Esther	Daniel	Galatians	1–2 Peter
1–2 Kings	Hosea	Ephesians	and Jude
Ezra and	Matthew	Philippians	Revelation
Nehemiah	Mark	Colossians and	
Job	Luke	Philemon	

•　　•　　•　　•　　•　　•

J. I. PACKER is Board of Governors' Professor of Theology at Regent College (Vancouver, BC). Dr. Packer earned his DPhil at the University of Oxford. He is known and loved worldwide as the author of the best-selling book *Knowing God*, as well as many other titles on theology and the Christian life. He serves as the General Editor of the ESV Bible and as the Theological Editor for the *ESV Study Bible*.

LANE T. DENNIS is President of Crossway, a not-for-profit publishing ministry. Dr. Dennis earned his PhD from Northwestern University. He is Chair of the ESV Bible Translation Oversight Committee and Executive Editor of the *ESV Study Bible*.

DANE C. ORTLUND is Executive Vice President of Bible Publishing and Bible Publisher at Crossway. He is a graduate of Covenant Theological Seminary (MDiv, ThM) and Wheaton College (BA, PhD). Dr. Ortlund has authored several books and scholarly articles in the areas of Bible, theology, and Christian living.

JAMES

A 12-WEEK STUDY

Greg Gilbert

WHEATON, ILLINOIS

Knowing the Bible: James, A 12-Week Study

Copyright © 2013 by Crossway

Published by Crossway
    1300 Crescent Street
    Wheaton, Illinois 60187

Some content used in this study guide has been adapted from the *ESV Study Bible* (Crossway), copyright 2008 by Crossway, pages 2387–2399. Used by permission. All rights reserved.

Cover design: Simplicated Studio

First printing 2013

Printed in the United States of America

All emphases in Scripture quotations have been added by the author.

Trade paperback ISBN: 978-1-4335-3479-9
PDF ISBN: 978-1-4335-3480-5
Mobipocket ISBN: 978-1-4335-3481-2
EPub ISBN: 978-1-4335-3482-9

Crossway is a publishing ministry of Good News Publishers.

VP			26	25	24	23	22	21	20	19	18	17
18	17	16	15	14	13	12	11	10	9	8	7	6

TABLE OF CONTENTS

KNOWING THE BIBLE, as the series title indicates, was created to help readers know and understand the meaning, the message, and the God of the Bible. Each volume in the series consists of 12 units that progressively take the reader through a clear, concise study of that book of the Bible. In this way, any given volume can fruitfully be used in a 12-week format either in group study, such as in a church-based context, or in individual study. Of course, these 12 studies could be completed in fewer or more than 12 weeks, as convenient, depending on the context in which they are used.

Each study unit gives an overview of the text at hand before digging into it with a series of questions for reflection or discussion. The unit then concludes by highlighting the gospel of grace in each passage ("Gospel Glimpses"), identifying whole-Bible themes that occur in the passage ("Whole-Bible Connections"), and pinpointing Christian doctrines that are affirmed in the passage ("Theological Soundings").

The final component to each unit is a section for reflecting on personal and practical implications from the passage at hand. The layout provides space for recording responses to the questions proposed, and we think readers need to do this to get the full benefit of the exercise. The series also includes definitions of key words. These definitions are indicated by a note number in the text and are found at the end of each chapter.

Lastly, for help in understanding the Bible in this deeper way, we would urge the reader to use the ESV Bible and the *ESV Study Bible*, which are available online at esv.org. The *Knowing the Bible* series is also available online. Additional 12-week studies covering each book of the Bible will be added as they become available.

May the Lord greatly bless your study as you seek to know him through knowing his Word.

J. I. Packer
Lane T. Dennis

WEEK 1: OVERVIEW

James's letter is one of the most quoted books of the entire Bible. It's filled with famous phrases and quotations that often make their way into Christian conversation:

- Faith produces steadfastness.
- God cannot be tempted.
- Every good and perfect gift comes from above.
- Be quick to hear, slow to speak, slow to anger.
- Be doers of the word, and not hearers only.
- Even the demons believe—and shudder!
- Faith apart from works is dead.
- Resist the devil and he will flee from you.

On the other hand, James is also full of passages that have left Christians scratching their heads. Does James have it in for rich people? What is the point of anointing a sick person with oil? Does James teach that if you just have enough faith, God will always heal? Then there are even larger and more pointed questions. Why doesn't James talk very much about the cross? Does he understand the gospel the same way the rest of the New Testament writers do? And isn't he disagreeing with Paul in chapter 2 about the relationship between faith, works, and salvation?

These are all important questions, and in the course of this study we'll address all of them. It helps, however, to realize that the primary message driving James's letter is that Christians' faith in the gospel should work itself out in a life of obedience. As he says in 1:22, believers in Jesus should not just *hear* the word and believe it, but they should also *do what it says*. The gospel of Jesus—which James understands deeply and affirms completely—results in a new life of obedience when a person believes. That's James's message, and as we come to understand that, his book will be a stirring exhortation to walk in a manner worthy of the calling to which we have been called.

Placing It in the Larger Story

James is an intensely practical book, filled with exhortations to Christians about the way they should live their lives now that they have been given new life in Jesus. It is filled with allusions to and quotations of the teaching of Jesus, and it includes more imperatives (commands) per word than any other New Testament book. For these reasons, James has been called "the Proverbs[1] of the New Testament."

James is therefore highly relevant to the Christian life. Unlike many of the other books of the New Testament, James's aim is not to give a theological presentation of the gospel. Rather, he writes his book to those who already believe the gospel, and his goal is to help them live faithfully as followers of Jesus. There are many different and seemingly disconnected themes in James—perseverance under trial, riches and poverty, wisdom, the danger of the tongue, prayer, and faith and works. But what ties them all together is James's desire to take the teaching of Jesus and apply it to the Christian's personal life.

Key Verse

"But be doers of the word, and not hearers only, deceiving yourselves." (James 1:22)

Date and Historical Background

The book of James was written by a man who identifies himself simply as "James, a servant of God and of the Lord Jesus Christ" (James 1:1). But who was this James? The very plainness of the address gives us some clue, because there were not many Jameses in the early church who could get away with such a simple identification. In fact, there was probably only one James who was famous enough to call himself simply "James" and expect that everyone would know who he was—James the brother of Jesus, the son of Mary and Joseph.

James died in AD 62, so the letter had to have been written before that. Further, if James wrote his letter after the Jerusalem council of AD 48–49, it's hard to imagine that he wouldn't have mentioned those events. Therefore, the book of James was almost certainly written in the mid-40s. That means that—despite the way the New Testament books are arranged—James likely wrote his book several years before Paul wrote his letters and only 15 years or so after Jesus had died and risen again.

James is a general epistle, meaning that it doesn't seem to be written to any particular church, but rather to all Christian churches in general. It is addressed to "the twelve tribes in the Dispersion,"[2] which probably means that James has Jewish Christians primarily in mind. The themes he addresses, however, are universal. Persevering under trial, not favoring the rich and powerful, taming the tongue—these are issues which will confront every Christian church and every believer.

Outline

   I. Greeting (1:1)

  II. The Testing of Faith (1:2–18)

 III. Hearing and Doing the Word (1:19–27)

 IV. The Sin of Partiality (2:1–13)

  V. Faith without Works Is Dead (2:14–25)

 VI. The Sin of Dissension in the Community (3:1–4:12)

VII. The Sins of the Wealthy (4:13–5:12)

VIII. The Prayer of Faith (5:13–18)

 IX. Concluding Admonition (5:19–20)

As You Get Started . . .

How have you thought about the book of James in the past? Does it confuse you, or have you found it helpful in your walk as a Christian?

After reading this introduction, why do you think James wrote his book? What is the main thing he's trying to accomplish in his readers' lives?

Why do you think James doesn't spend time giving a systematic presentation of the gospel? How is his aim different from Paul's aim in, say, Romans or Galatians?

Which parts of James most perplex or confuse you? Are there any parts of the book to which you want to give special attention as you begin this study?

> ### As You Finish This Unit . . .

Take a moment now to ask for the Lord's blessing and help as you engage in this study of James. And take a moment also to look back through this unit of study, to reflect on a few key things that you would like to learn throughout this study of James.

Definitions

[1] **Proverb** – A brief saying that conveys a lesson about how to live wisely and well, usually drawn from observations about nature and life. The book of Proverbs contains the vast majority of biblical proverbs, but they occur in other books as well.

[2] **Dispersion** – From the Greek for "scattering," refers to the numerous relocations of large groups of Israelites/Jews throughout the world, including to Assyria and Media (722 BC), Babylon (586), Alexandria in Egypt (c. 300), Phrygia (c. 200), and Rome (c. 63). This dispersion resulted in greater exposure of the Jews to other peoples and also laid the groundwork for the worldwide spread of the gospel during the first century.

Week 2: The Testing of Faith

James 1:1–11

The Place of the Passage

James opens with an exhortation to his readers to persevere under trial. As those who are dispersed throughout the world, sometimes even by persecution, they are hard-pressed on every side. James encourages his readers to realize that one important mark of the Christian life is to trust God rather than self—even when life seems unbearably hard. If you do that, he says, God will use your trials to make you a more faithful follower of Jesus.

The Big Picture

James tells his readers not to despair because of their trials, but rather to bear up under them, relying on God, recognizing that he is using their trials for their good.

> ### Reflection and Discussion

Read through the complete passage for this study, James 1:1–11. Then review the shorter passages below and write your own notes on the following questions. (For further background, see the *ESV Study Bible*, page 2391, also available online at esv.org.)

1. Joy in Trials (1:1–4)

James identifies himself as "a servant of God and of the Lord Jesus Christ." Knowing that James would have grown up with Jesus—known him as a child, a teenager, a young adult—does it seem remarkable to you that James would now call his brother "Lord"[1] and "Christ"?[2] What do you think happened that convinced James that Jesus, his crucified brother, is here and now the Lord and Messiah?[3]

James addresses his letter "to the twelve tribes in the Dispersion," but he is not writing only to Jewish believers. He is alluding to the fact that just as the children of Israel were dispersed throughout the world in their exile, so also believers in Christ are now aliens and strangers who are waiting for God to gather them home to himself (see also 1 Pet. 1:1; 2:11). What, then, is the connection between verses 1 and 2? How does a reminder to Christians of their status as aliens and strangers in this world set up James's exhortation to them to "count it all joy" when they meet trials?

Verses 2–4 are a chain argument in which one thing leads to another. Trace the chain that James describes. What is the end result of our trials?

The word translated "steadfastness" in verse 3 literally means "to remain under," like a person holding up a heavy weight for a long period of time. Think of someone who lifts weights for exercise. What is the "full effect" of that person's "steadfastness?" What are some of the effects of our remaining steadfast under the weight of trials?

2. Wisdom from God in Trials (1:5–8)

The exhortation in verse 5 to ask God for wisdom is not disconnected from the theme of persevering under trials. Read Proverbs 2:1–15. What is wisdom? Where does it come from? What are the benefits of having wisdom?

As in the Old Testament, wisdom is a God-given and God-centered discernment regarding God's world and how best to live in it. In other words, it is seeing the world and your circumstances as God sees them and then acting in accord with that knowledge. How, then, does God see our trials in this life? How is that different from the way we are tempted to see them? If we could understand our trials as God understands them, how would we act differently?

The word translated "doubt" in verse 6 is literally "dispute." It is used in many different contexts to refer to a dispute with another person. Here, though, James uses the word to refer to a person disputing within one's own self! In other words, to *doubt* is to be a person of a fundamentally divided mind and a fundamentally inconsistent attitude toward God. It's a reckless and wavering distrust—a *refusal* finally to trust God. The point is not that a Christian never has doubts; it's that a Christian never allows his mind to become so divided and self-disputing that it *welcomes* those doubts. A Christian will always strive to take the side of God and truth against doubts when they arise. What are some strategies Christians can use to fight doubt? How can you resist becoming "a double-minded person, unstable in all your ways?"

---

3. Don't Trust in Yourself, No Matter Your Station in Life (1:9–11)

James has much to say in his book about poverty and wealth, and how God expects us to use the resources he gives us. Most of the time in this book, the wealthy are evil people who are oppressing James's readers (e.g., 2:6 and 5:1–5). But is that always true? Read 4:13–15. James is speaking here to a group of relatively wealthy businesspeople who are traveling to another city in order to make a profit. But it also seems that these businesspeople might be believers! Here's why: When James addresses wicked, rich oppressors, he doesn't exhort them to do anything; he simply condemns them. Here, though, he treats these businesspeople as Christians, teaching them to adjust their thinking and their speech to fit true theology. So does James set up a simplistic "poor equals righteous, rich equals wicked" equation? Does the rest of the Bible? What is the Bible's general opinion of wealth—that it is evil, or that it is dangerous? What other passages of Scripture support your answer?

In verses 9–11, James points out our universal tendency to boast in ourselves and to rely on our own accomplishments. Both rich people and poor people have this tendency, so James addresses them both. He exhorts the poor person to boast in his "exaltation"—that is, in what God has done in Christ—rather than to despair because of poverty. And he exhorts the rich person to boast in his or her "humiliation"—that is, in his or her identification with the suffering Christ—and not in riches, because the riches will soon pass away. How does material wealth tend to lead to self-reliance? Does material poverty *always* lead to reliance on God? If not, what kinds of things can it lead a person wrongly to rely on?

What kinds of things besides wealth do we tend to rely on and boast in for a sense of well-being and security, rather than on God?

For each of the things you mentioned in the previous question, explain why it is foolish to rely on them. Why is it better and wiser to rely on God?

Read through the following three sections on *Gospel Glimpses, Whole-Bible Connections,* and *Theological Soundings.* Then take time to reflect on the *Personal Implications* these sections may have for your walk with the Lord.

▶ Gospel Glimpses

A SERVANT OF JESUS CHRIST. Some readers think that the letter of James barely qualifies as a Christian book because it doesn't give a systematic presentation of the gospel. That, however, is to misunderstand what James is doing. He is writing his book to people who already understand the gospel, and he is helping them to see how to live in a way that reflects their faith in Jesus. James understands very well the truth of the gospel and of Jesus' identity. Even in his very first line, he identifies himself as a servant of Jesus *the Christ.* That is not Jesus' last name! It is a theologically rich title that identifies Jesus as the promised Messiah—the king who would save his people from their sins.

AN UNWAVERING FAITH. The fundamental call of the gospel is for us to "repent[4] and believe" (Mark 1:15). In other words, we are to put our faith[5] in Jesus—to rely on him and trust him. James calls for exactly that kind of faith in this section of his book. True faith in Christ is not a faith that hedges its bets—"I'll rely 90 percent on Jesus, but 10 percent on my own righteousness."

Authentic faith is not divided, double-minded, and unstable. It's a faith that gives itself wholly to Jesus, relying on him and him alone for salvation.

BOASTING IN CHRIST. James says that whether we are rich or poor, our only boast should be in what God has done for us. He makes the point with rich irony. Whereas the world sees the poor as contemptible, they should boast that God has exalted them in Christ. And whereas the world sees the rich as honorable, they should boast that God has humbled them and shown them their need for salvation. Paul says something very similar in Galatians 6:14 when he writes, "Far be it from me to boast except in the cross of our Lord Jesus Christ, by which the world has been crucified to me, and I to the world."

> ## Whole-Bible Connections

THE TWELVE TRIBES IN THE DISPERSION. Centuries before the birth of Jesus, the twelve tribes of Israel were exiled from their land and scattered among the nations of the world. The northern kingdom was carried into exile by the Assyrian empire, and the southern kingdom was exiled by the Babylonian empire. The Old Testament prophets held out the hope that one day God would return his people to their land and restore them (Jer. 31:7–14; Ezek. 37:15–28). During their exile, however, they had to endure as aliens and strangers. The New Testament applies those same categories to believers in Christ. Peter, for example, addresses his first letter to the "elect exiles of the Dispersion" (1 Pet. 1:1). Like God's people centuries ago, we Christians are a people waiting for our final redemption when Jesus returns.

THE BENEFIT OF TRIALS. The New Testament is very clear that believers will face trials of many kinds. Just as our Lord was tested in the wilderness (Matt. 4:1–11), and just as he endured temptation (Heb. 4:15), so we too are called to endure trial and temptation in this life. However, the Bible also promises us that God will use our trials for our good, strengthening us and leading us to rely more fully on him. Paul makes a similar point in Romans 5:3–5, and Peter too compares the effect of trials on our faith to the way fire purifies gold (1 Pet. 1:7).

WISDOM FROM GOD. The book of Proverbs tells us that wisdom comes only from God himself (Prov. 2:6). It also tells us that wisdom existed before the world was created (Prov. 8:22–23), and that it is the *order* according to which he created the world (Prov. 8:27–31). Wisdom, therefore, is much more than we usually think. It is not just pithy sayings or clever solutions to problems. It is actually the very mind of God, the pattern according to which he created and ordered the world. To have wisdom, therefore, is to see the world as God sees it, and then to act in accordance with that understanding. And of course, how has God most fully and completely revealed his mind and character to us? Through his Son, Jesus Christ, the incarnate[6] Word of God.

Theological Soundings

JESUS AS CHRIST. James bases his entire book on his confession of Jesus as the Christ (1:1). He understands his brother to be the long-awaited Messiah, with all that entails. Jesus is the King who had come to inaugurate God's kingdom,[7] but he is also the King who would suffer in the place of his people in order to qualify them to share in that kingdom.

THE GOODNESS OF GOD. James says that God "gives generously" to those who ask him. The Bible's consistent witness is that God is unspeakably generous and merciful. From his mercy to Adam, to his rescue of Noah from the flood, to his choosing of Israel to be his special people, God proves himself to be a good God, not a stingy and grasping one.

HUMANS ARE MORTAL. Our physical lives do not last forever. Just as the grass withers and the flower fades, so we are here one moment and gone the next. That reality powerfully underlines James's main point—that our faith should be not in our own wavering, unstable selves, but in the unchanging and immortal God.

Personal Implications

Take time to reflect on the implications of James 1:1–11 for your own life today. Make notes below on the personal implications for your walk with the Lord of (1) the *Gospel Glimpses*, (2) the *Whole-Bible Connections*, (3) the *Theological Soundings*, and (4) this passage as a whole.

1. Gospel Glimpses

2. Whole-Bible Connections

3. Theological Soundings

----

4. James 1:1–11

As You Finish This Unit . . .

Take a moment now to ask for the Lord's blessing and help as you engage in this study of James. And take a moment also to look back through this unit of study, to reflect on a few key things that the Lord may be teaching you—and perhaps to highlight or underline these to review again in the future.

Definitions

[1] **Lord** – Someone superior in authority or status to another, similar to "master." It is a common translation for several different Hebrew titles for God in the OT, and in the NT refers to Jesus, who is enthroned as ruler of the kingdom of God.

[2] **Christ** – Transliteration of the Greek for "Anointed One" (equivalent to Hebrew Messiah). The term is used throughout the NT as a title for Jesus, indicating his role as Messiah and Savior.

[3] **Messiah** – Transliteration of a Hebrew word meaning "Anointed One," the equivalent of the Greek word Christ. Originally applied to anyone specially designated for a particular role, such as king or priest. Jesus himself affirmed that he was the Messiah sent from God (Matt. 16:16–17).

[4] **Repentance** – A complete change of heart and mind regarding one's overall attitude toward God and one's individual actions. True regeneration and conversion is always accompanied by repentance.

[5] **Faith** – Trust in or reliance upon something or someone deemed trustworthy despite a lack of concrete proof. Salvation, which is purely a work of God's grace, can be received only through faith (Rom. 5:2; Eph. 2:8–9).

[6] **Incarnation** – Literally "(becoming) in flesh," this word, formed from Latin, refers to God becoming a human being in the person of Jesus of Nazareth.

[7] **Kingdom of God/heaven** – The sovereign rule of God. At the present time, the fallen, sinful world does not belong to the kingdom of God, since it does not submit to God's rule. Instead, God's kingdom can be found in heaven and among his people on earth (Matt. 6:9–10; Luke 17:20–21). After Christ returns, however, the kingdom of the world will become the kingdom of God (Rev. 11:15). Then all people will, either willingly or regretfully, acknowledge his sovereignty (Phil. 2:9–11). Even the natural world will be transformed to operate in perfect harmony with God (Rom. 8:19–23).

Week 3: The Process of Temptation

James 1:12–18

The Place of the Passage

Having encouraged his readers to endure trials with perseverance and stead-fastness, James now begins to teach them that they should not blame God for the temptations with which they struggle. On the contrary, God is infinitely good and faithful. He does not change, he is not capricious, and he gives good gifts to his children. Just look at what he has done for you, James says, in giving you new spiritual life! No, the sins you face—and commit—result from your own heart being enticed and lured away by evil desires. So stand firm, he tells them, because when the test is over, reward is waiting!

The Big Picture

James 1:12–18 shows us how our hearts respond sinfully to temptation and directs us not to blame God for our sins, but to find strength in his goodness and grace.

Reflection and Discussion

Read through the complete passage for this study, James 1:12–18. Then review the shorter passages below and write your own notes on the following questions. (For further background, see the *ESV Study Bible*, page 2392, also available online at esv.org.)

1. Reward for Those Who Endure (1:12)

What is the reward that James promises will come to those who steadfastly endure trials? Can you think of other passages of Scripture that point to similar rewards?

How should the promise of reward for endurance motivate us in our walk with Christ?

2. The Process of Temptation (1:13–15)

We often read 1:12–13 as if James is moving from one topic to a wholly different one—as if he has been talking about trials but is now moving on to talk about temptation. The two concepts are tightly related, however, because trials in our lives will always lead us to temptation. Financial struggle, for example, leads us to distrust God. Stress tempts us to be selfish. Name some specific trials that you have experienced, and consider the sins that you were tempted to fall into because of those trials.

The Bible teaches that God often, in his providence,[1] ordains that his people should face trials. What passages of Scripture teach that truth? What stories in the Bible illustrate it?

If God sometimes ordains that his people will face trials, what then is James saying in verse 13 that God does *not* do? (Hint: there is a difference between trial and temptation! See the note on verse 13 in the *ESV Study Bible*.)

In verses 14–15 James uses two metaphors to describe the process of temptation and sin in our hearts. The first, in verse 14, is an image from fishing. Temptation "entices" a person to bite down on sin, and then when the hook is set, he or she is "dragged away." That is a terrifying thought. We see the pleasure of sin, are enticed by it, and then before we even realize it, we have lost all control and sin is dragging us away. How have you seen that process of temptation, enticement, sin, and dragging away play out in your own life?

The second metaphor James uses is one of conception and birth. What does it mean for a desire to "conceive?"

When once we act on our evil desires and give birth to sin, what does James say is the end result after sin "is fully grown?"

3. God's Goodness and Faithfulness (1:16–18)

Why does James turn in verse 16 to talk about God's goodness and faithfulness? What are his readers in danger of deceiving themselves about, with particular reference to their trials and the temptations that come with them?

With what do you think James is contrasting God when he says that "with [him] there is no variation or shadow due to change?"

What does it mean to be "brought forth?" Has James used this metaphor before in this chapter? Read John 3:1–6. Where did James get this idea of Christians having been "brought forth?"

_____

_____

_____

_____

_____

_____

What is the "word of truth?" If we are brought forth "by the word of truth," do you think it's possible for a person to be saved apart from the gospel?

_____

_____

_____

_____

_____

James's point in verse 18 is to show his readers that God is good and that he gives good gifts. How does his example of the gift of regeneration[2] accomplish that goal? (Read Romans 8:32. James is using the same kind of reasoning.)

_____

_____

_____

_____

_____

Read through the following three sections on *Gospel Glimpses*, *Whole-Bible Connections*, and *Theological Soundings*. Then take time to reflect on the *Personal Implications* these sections may have for your walk with the Lord.

Gospel Glimpses

THE WORD OF TRUTH. James is very clear that salvation comes through the message of the gospel, that is, the word of truth about Jesus and his work on our behalf. Paul uses the same phrase in Ephesians 1:13 when he says that those believers were sealed with the Holy Spirit when they heard "the word of truth." He even explains what he means by "word of truth," calling it "the gospel of your salvation." Salvation comes when a person hears the message about Jesus and responds to it with faith and repentance.

BROUGHT US FORTH. One of the clearest characteristics of James's book is how much he learned from Jesus. His teaching can almost always be traced directly back to the explicit teaching of the Lord. This metaphor of salvation as birth, for example, finds its roots in Jesus' teaching about the new birth in John 3. Becoming a Christian is not just a moral decision or "turning over a new leaf." It is a radical change of one's heart—a gift of new spiritual life where there was once only death. God is the giver of life, both physical and spiritual.

OF HIS OWN WILL. James is in agreement with the rest of the New Testament that salvation is not finally attributable to human will or action, but rather to God's own will and mere mercy.[3] John makes this clear in John 1:13 when he says that salvation is "not . . . of the will of the flesh nor of the will of man, but of God." Paul says the same thing in Romans 9:16 when he teaches, "So then it depends not on human will or exertion, but on God, who has mercy." Our salvation is wholly of grace.[4] It is not deserved, and it is not earned. God gives it to us as a gift—of his own will.

Whole-Bible Connections

FATHER OF LIGHTS. James traces God's goodness—his desire to give good gifts—all the way back to creation. At every stage in his creating of the universe, God declares that his work is good. That reveals something to us not only about the universe that God made but also about the character of God himself. He *is* good, and therefore he *does* good! Throughout the Bible, believers confess this to be true. Joseph affirms it even in the midst of his trials (Gen. 50:20), the Israelites confessed it as they looked into the Promised Land (Deut. 26:11), and the psalmists said it over and over (Ps. 73:1 and 84:11, for example). We do not serve a grudging, stingy God, but a good and generous one!

FIRSTFRUITS OF HIS CREATURES. James may have in mind here the fact that his readers were some of the first people in the world to receive the gospel of Jesus Christ. Other New Testament writings take special note of those who were "first" in believing (Rom. 16:5; 1 Cor. 16:15). But James may also be looking forward to the last day, when God will create a new heaven and a new earth. As the crowning act of God's work of creation (Gen. 1:26–31), it is fitting that humans should be the "firstfruits"—the down payment, as it were—on the re-creation of the cosmos. Paul seems to teach this when he says in Romans 8:19–21 that the creation "waits with eager longing for the revealing of the sons of God," because in that last day creation will share in "the freedom of the glory of the children of God." Our salvation in Christ is the firstfruits—the crowning act of and the down payment on—God's universe-encompassing work of redemption.

Theological Soundings

GOD AS CREATOR. James reminds us that everything begins with God. He is the Creator, the Father of lights, and the originator of everything that exists. In fact, the Bible teaches that God created the world *ex nihilo*, or "out of nothing." He did not take preexisting material and form it into something else, nor did he simply bring "order out of chaos." Interestingly, that is what the *pagan* deities were said to have done. But the Bible is clear that our God is no pagan deity. He did not just bring order out of chaos; he brought *everything* out of *nothing*. He is the Father of it all.

GOD IS HOLY. When James says that God cannot be tempted by evil, he affirms that God is holy[5] and pure and perfectly righteous. God is not a mixture of good and evil motives, good and evil desires. Without fail and without exception, he is holy and good.

GOD TESTS, BUT DOES NOT TEMPT. The Bible is very clear that God does sometimes *test* his people. He tests Abraham, for example, when he tells him in Genesis 22 that he is to sacrifice his son Isaac. He also tests his people Israel in the wilderness to see whether they would obey his commands (Ex. 16:4). But God does not tempt his people to evil. When we are tempted in the midst of our trials, that is the result of our own sinful hearts, and the question is whether we will remain steadfast and endure our trials in faith, or give in to temptation and sin.

Personal Implications

Take time to reflect on the implications of James 1:12–18 for your own life today. Make notes below on the personal implications for your walk with the Lord of (1) the *Gospel Glimpses*, (2) the *Whole-Bible Connections*, (3) the *Theological Soundings*, and (4) this passage as a whole.

1. Gospel Glimpses

2. Whole-Bible Connections

3. Theological Soundings

4. James 1:12–18

> ## As You Finish This Unit . . .

Take a moment now to ask for the Lord's blessing and help as you engage in this study of James. And take a moment also to look back through this unit of study, to reflect on a few key things that the Lord may be teaching you—and perhaps to highlight or underline these to review again in the future.

Definitions

[1] **Providence** – God's good, wise, and sovereign guidance and control of all things, by which he supplies all our needs and accomplishes his holy will.

[2] **Regeneration** – The Holy Spirit's work of bringing spiritual life to a person, thus enabling him or her to love and follow God. Essentially equivalent to what is often referred to as being "born again" or "saved."

[3] **Mercy** – Compassion and kindness toward someone experiencing hardship, sometimes even when such suffering results from the person's own sin or foolishness. God displays mercy toward his people and they, in turn, are called to display mercy toward others (Luke 6:36).

[4] **Grace** – Unmerited favor, especially the free gift of salvation that God gives to believers through faith in Jesus Christ.

[5] **Holiness** – A quality possessed by something or someone set apart for special use. When applied to God, it refers to his utter perfection and complete transcendence over creation. God's people are called to imitate his holiness (Lev. 19:2), which means being set apart from sin and reserved for his purposes.

Week 4: Hearing and Doing the Word

James 1:19–27

The Place of the Passage

In 1:19 James turns to the main point he wants to make in his letter—that Christianity is not just about believing certain things or claiming to have faith; it is having your life transformed by the gospel. In other words, being a Christian is not just about hearing God's word, but also doing it. Of course, that doesn't mean that hearing the word isn't important. A mind that is discontent, full of its own opinions, and not ready to listen will not be able to receive God's word. But once the word is received, it must be put into action. That, finally, is the mark of a Christian.

The Big Picture

As Christians, we should not only hear the word of God, but also put it into practice.

> ## Reflection and Discussion

Read through the complete passage for this study, James 1:19–27. Then review the shorter passages below and write your own notes on the following questions. (For further background, see the *ESV Study Bible*, pages 2392–2393, also available online at esv.org.)

1. Hearers of the Word (1:19–21)

Reading through the book of James, it is easy to think that he is moralistic in his understanding of what it means to be a Christian. In other words, one can have the impression that he thinks a right relationship with God is all about doing this or doing that. That, however, is a wrong impression. With all his moral instruction and ethical exhortation, James is not telling a person how to become a Christian. How do you know that's the case? To whom does James address the moral instruction that begins in 1:19?

If James is speaking to "beloved brothers" beginning in 1:19, and if *doing* is not what makes a person a Christian, what then *is* it that makes a person a Christian? (Hint: look back at 1:18.)

There is a common line of reasoning in Scripture[1] that runs from the new birth to the putting off of evil. Paul follows that line of reasoning in Romans 6:1–14, and Peter follows it also in 1 Peter 1:1–23. Does James make the same argument? In what verse does he talk about the new birth? In what verse does he talk about "putting away" evil as a result of that new birth?

What kind of mindset does it take to receive the word of God? How would *slowness* to hear, *quickness* to speak, and *quickness* to anger hinder the word from taking root in a person's heart?

----

2. Doers of the Word (1:22–25)

Verse 22 is perhaps the best candidate for a "topic sentence" of James's letter. More than any other verse, it encapsulates the message James wants to get across to his readers. In fact, the rest of the book will unpack this message of *doing* the word—not just *hearing* it—by looking at a number of issues with which James's readers seem to be struggling. Look through the rest of the book of James. What kinds of issues do you see James addressing? Explain how each is a matter of putting God's word into practice

----

What metaphor does James use to describe a person who only hears the word, but does not do it? What kinds of things characterize a person who would look in a mirror and then immediately forget what he sees (e.g., impatience, refusal to focus, etc.)?

In verse 25 James refers to "the perfect law," and then explains what he means by calling it "the law of liberty." What do you think this "perfect law" is? (See the note on 1:25 in the *ESV Study Bible*.)

----

3. True, Practical Religion (1:26–27)

These verses are often used to say that the essence of Christianity is to live a moral life—in other words, that if you simply do these things, you will be saved. Is that a correct understanding of what James is saying here? How do you know?

James gives three examples in these verses of what it means to *do* the Word. What are they? (Hint: there is one in verse 26 and two in verse 27.)

James uses these three particular examples, probably not to say that they are the only fruits of a life transformed by the word of truth, nor even that they are the most important. After all, the New Testament mentions many different fruits that come from a transformed life. Rather, he probably uses them for two reasons: first, because each of these fruits has a long pedigree in Old Testament teaching; and second, because they seem to be particular struggles of James's readers. Find one or two Old Testament passages that teach these same things, and then look through James and find where he addresses each of these ideas again.

Read through the following three sections on *Gospel Glimpses*, *Whole-Bible Connections*, and *Theological Soundings*. Then take time to reflect on the *Personal Implications* these sections may have for your walk with the Lord.

Gospel Glimpses

MY BELOVED BROTHERS. "Brothers" is a term that Christians used for one another to refer to their mutual union with Christ and their inclusion in God's family. It is a natural companion to Christians' practice—taught by Jesus in his prayer in Matthew 6—of calling God their "Father." James's use of the term here shows us that he is addressing his book to people who are already Christians. He is not telling them what it takes to bring one into a relationship with God. Rather, he's telling them what a life transformed by the word of truth will look like. The new birth that God gives will issue in a life of obedience.

THE IMPLANTED WORD IS ABLE TO SAVE YOUR SOULS. Again, James affirms his understanding that it is the word of the gospel that saves.

Whole-Bible Connections

THE WISDOM OF HEARING, SPEAKING, AND ANGER. James draws heavily on Old Testament Wisdom Literature throughout his book—especially

Proverbs and Ecclesiastes. His exhortations to be quick to hear, slow to speak, and slow to anger so that we may be ready to receive the Word of God have deep roots in Wisdom Literature. Ecclesiastes 5:2, for example, says, "Be not rash with your mouth, nor let your heart be hasty to utter a word before God, for God is in heaven and you are on earth. Therefore let your words be few." Proverbs 10:19 says, "When words are many, transgression is not lacking, but whoever restrains his lips is prudent."

THE IMPLANTED WORD. One of the great promises God made to his people regarding the new covenant is that his word would no longer be written on stone tablets, but rather would take up residence in their hearts. In Jeremiah 31:33 he says, "For this is the covenant that I will make with the house of Israel after those days, declares the LORD: I will put my law within them, and I will write it on their hearts." God also declares in Ezekiel 11:19–20: "I will remove the heart of stone from their flesh and give them a heart of flesh, that they may walk in my statutes and keep my rules and obey them." With his reference to "the implanted word," James is picking up on one of God's most exhilarating promises to renew and save his people!

VISIT ORPHANS AND WIDOWS. One of God's most celebrated characteristics in the Old Testament is his particular concern for those who are most helpless. Moreover, because he shows that kind of concern, he expects his people to do the same. We can see this very clearly in Deuteronomy 10:18–19. Speaking of God, Moses says, "He executes justice for the fatherless and the widow, and loves the sojourner, giving him food and clothing." And that description of God is followed immediately by this command: "Love the sojourner, therefore, for you were sojourners in the land of Egypt." The point is simple but crucial: The people of God should be like God.

Theological Soundings

THE FATHERHOOD OF GOD AND BROTHERHOOD OF MAN? Some Christians have used the language of "brotherhood" to refer to all of human-ity, regardless of whether a person is a believer in Christ. After all, they reason, God is the father of all by virtue of his having created us all. It's easy to see the logic at work in that argument, but that is not how the Bible uses the term "brother." "Brother" and "sister" are terms of address reserved for those who are also united to Christ by faith (and, of course, for those who are blood rela-tives). Moreover, to call God "Father" is the special privilege of those who are reconciled[2] to him through Christ and adopted[3] into his family.

PAST, PRESENT, AND FUTURE SALVATION. James says that the implanted word is "able to save your souls." That is a very interesting way of talking to Christians! After all, aren't they *already* saved? What does James mean by referring to a future salvation? Actually, the Bible uses all three tenses—past, present, and future—to refer to God's work of salvation in our lives. We *have been* saved (Eph. 2:5), we *are being* saved (1 Cor. 15:2), and we *will be* saved in the end (Matt. 10:22). God's work of salvation is all-encompassing, including justification,[4] sanctification,[5] and glorification[6] (Rom. 8:29–30).

Personal Implications

Take time to reflect on the implications of James 1:19–27 for your own life today. Make notes below on the personal implications for your walk with the Lord of (1) the *Gospel Glimpses*, (2) the *Whole-Bible Connections*, (3) the *Theological Soundings*, and (4) this passage as a whole.

1. Gospel Glimpses

2. Whole-Bible Connections

3. Theological Soundings

4. James 1:19–27

As You Finish This Unit . . .

Take a moment now to ask for the Lord's blessing and help as you engage in this study of James. And take a moment also to look back through this unit of study, to reflect on a few key things that the Lord may be teaching you—and perhaps to highlight or underline these to review again in the future.

Definitions

[1] **Scripture** – Writings regarded by Christians as inspired by God and authoritative in all areas of doctrine and practice.

[2] **Reconciliation** – The restoration of relationship and peace between alienated or opposing parties. Through his death and resurrection, Jesus has reconciled believers to God (2 Cor. 5:18–21).

[3] **Adoption** – Legal process by which a person gives the status of a son or daughter to another person who is not his or her child by birth. The NT uses the term to describe the act by which God makes believers his children through the atoning death and resurrection of his one and only true Son, Jesus (see Romans 8; Galatians 4).

[4] **Justification** – The act of God's grace in bringing sinners into a new covenant relationship with himself and counting them as righteous before him through the forgiveness of sins (Rom. 3:20–26).

[5] **Sanctification** – The process of being conformed to the image of Jesus Christ through the work of the Holy Spirit. This process begins immediately after regeneration and continues throughout a Christian's life.

[6] **Glorification** – The work of God in believers to bring them to the ultimate and perfect stage of salvation— Christlikeness—following his justification and sanctification of them (Rom. 8:29– 30). Glorification includes believers receiving imperishable resurrection bodies at Christ's return (1 Cor. 15:42–44).

WEEK 5: THE SIN OF PARTIALITY

James 2:1–13

The Place of the Passage

At the beginning of chapter 2, James turns to address a particular failing among his readers in their doing of the word. Far from being a people characterized by a genuine love and concern for the helpless (1:27), they have actually fallen into showing partiality to the rich and powerful. James is appalled by this behavior—first, because it is so diametrically opposed to God's character; second, because it puts these Christians in the position of acting just like the ungodly world; and third, because it is a violation of our King's law! These believers' behavior is no small issue. It puts them at odds with God's law, and therefore with God himself.

The Big Picture

In their relationships with other people, Christians ought to be driven by a set of values and principles—in a word, love—that is radically different from the world.

> ## Reflection and Discussion

Read through the complete passage for this study, James 2:1–13. Then review the shorter passages below and write your own notes on the following questions. (For further background, see the *ESV Study Bible*, pages 2393–2394, also available online at esv.org.)

1. Preferring the Wealthy over the Poor (2:1–4)

Read verses 1–4. What is the particular problem that James is addressing among these believers?

Why do you think these believers would act in this way? Why would they show partiality to the rich and powerful?

What does James want his readers to do instead of showing partiality to the rich and powerful? Does he want them to show partiality to the poor? Read 2:1 carefully!

Why does James think it is so bad to make "distinctions among yourselves?" Read Ephesians 4:1–3 and 1 Peter 3:8 before you answer.

Do you remember James's teaching in 1:6–8 about "doubting?" The word "doubt" there meant something like "self-disputing," or being divided against oneself, turned against oneself. Well, the word "distinctions" here in 2:4 is the same word. How does that idea of being *divided* and *turned against oneself* help you understand why it is so bad to have such "distinctions" created in the church?

----

2. Three Reasons Why Showing Partiality Is Ungodly (2:5–13)

In verse 5, James gives the first of three reasons for why showing partiality to the rich and powerful is wrong. It is, simply, that to do so is utterly unlike God! While these Christians are genuflecting before the rich and powerful, James says, God has chosen to give the gifts of faith and the kingdom to those who are poor in the world's eyes. In fact, God has a long history in the Old Testament of showing special care and concern for the poor. Can you find some passages in the Old Testament that show this?

Think more about God's special concern for the poor, shown in the Old Testament. Why does he do this? Read Psalm 10:12–14. You see? It is those who are *helpless* to whom God shows special concern—those who are marked by a recognition that they cannot help themselves. And throughout Scripture, poverty tends toward that kind of humility more than wealth does. In the same way, sickness tends toward humility more than health. That's why Jesus said, "Those who are well have no need of a physician, but those who are sick" (Matt. 9:12). Can you see in your own life how wealth, health, or other strengths lead you to rely on those things rather than on God? Explain how that works in your experience. Explain, too, how weaknesses lead you to humbly lean on God.

Is James saying here that being materially poor automatically results in salvation? Look carefully at verse 5. To whom has God promised the kingdom? To "those who have little money"?

In verses 8–9 James gives a third reason why showing partiality to the rich and powerful is wrong: It is a violation of the King's law. The word "royal" is important in understanding *which* body of law James is referring to. It is not the Old Testament law in itself, but rather the Old Testament law *as interpreted and fulfilled by King Jesus*. That's what makes the law royal; it belongs to the King! Can you think of some Scriptures where Jesus claims the right to interpret the Old Testament law—that is, to say what it actually means?

James says that the royal law accords with the commandment "You shall love your neighbor as yourself." In other words, that commandment encapsulates and sums up the law that King Jesus gives to his people. Why does James choose that particular commandment as the "summing up" one? Does he pick it at random out of all the commandments Jesus gives, or does Jesus himself give it some special status? (Hint: read Matthew 22:36–40.)

In verses 10–11, why is it true that breaking one commandment of the law makes a person accountable for the whole law?

Read through the following three sections on *Gospel Glimpses, Whole-Bible Connections*, and *Theological Soundings*. Then take time to reflect on the *Personal Implications* these sections may have for your walk with the Lord.

Gospel Glimpses

THE KINGDOM PROMISED TO THOSE WHO LOVE HIM. James is sometimes accused of not understanding the gospel, and of believing that salvation is granted to those who are poor *simply* by virtue of their being poor. It really would be hard to misunderstand James any more! We've already seen that James understands very well that salvation comes "by the word of truth" (1:18), and now here in 2:5 he says that the kingdom is promised to those who love God. It is not poverty itself that secures salvation; it is faith and trust in God through Christ—though James recognizes that material poverty can sometimes lead to that kind of humility more easily than can material wealth.

RICH IN FAITH. James is also accused sometimes of disparaging the importance of faith. We will consider that idea more in the next section, but even here in verse 5, we see that James understands well the importance of faith. We are to be rich in it!

MERCY TRIUMPHS OVER JUDGMENT. In verse 13, James appeals to the mercy God has shown to us in order to motivate our own obedience. Salvation,[1] once again, is not a matter of doing enough to earn God's favor. It is a matter of his mercy in Christ. He does not give us what we deserve for our sin. Because of that, our own lives should be marked by mercy as well. As we interact with people, our sinful hearts inevitably desire to judge and create divisions, to separate and push away. But mercy, James exhorts, should triumph over judgment, just as it did in our own case before God.

Whole-Bible Connections

THE LORD OF GLORY. James tells his readers in 2:1 that Jesus Christ is "the Lord of Glory." Paul uses the same title for him in 1 Corinthians 2:8. *Glory* is an important term in the Old Testament, for it characterizes God himself. When God spoke to Israel out of the fire on Mount Sinai, Moses said, "Behold, the LORD our God has shown us his glory and greatness, and we have heard his voice out of the midst of the fire" (Deut. 5:24). The Psalms repeatedly refer to "the God of glory." All this makes it nothing short of amazing that the early Christians could say something like, "And the Word became flesh and dwelt among us, and we have seen his glory, glory as of the only Son from the Father" (John 1:14). By applying the title "Lord of glory" to Jesus, James is likewise strongly affirming his divinity.

THE ROYAL LAW. In Matthew 5, Jesus claimed to have the right to interpret God's law—that is, to say what it meant. The symbolism there is striking. Just as Moses went up on a mountain to receive the law that God would give, so Jesus stands on a mountain to deliver his Sermon on the Mount. He is the divine Lawgiver, and he alone has the right to interpret the law. James recognizes this in his phrase "the royal law." He is not referring to the Old Testament law as such, but rather to that law as interpreted and fulfilled by King Jesus.

Theological Soundings

ACT AS THOSE WHO ARE TO BE JUDGED. Christians do not live in fear that they will be condemned by God. After all, "there is therefore now no condemnation for those who are in Christ Jesus" (Rom. 8:1). Nevertheless, the Bible promises that Christians will give an account of their lives at the final judgment[2] (1 Cor. 3:12–15; 2 Cor. 5:10). This need not create anxiety in the hearts of believers, for Christ's righteousness covers all our failures. But the reality of the inevitable final judgment is sobering for us all, and also heartening in that it assures us that all wrongs will be made right someday.

THE LAW OF LIBERTY. One of the main blessings of being a Christian is that it brings freedom from the law. That does not mean that Christians do not live under a law at all. On the contrary, as James affirms, we live under the royal law of King Jesus. But there is something fascinating about that law: it is a law of liberty, not of slavery. As Paul says in Galatians 5:1, "Christ has set us free!" What he means is that we no longer relate to the law as slaves, obeying it out of fear of punishment. Rather, we relate to our King's royal law as heirs and sons, obeying it out of love for the King himself and a desire to live lives that will honor him. Our obedience is not one of slavery, but one of freedom!

Personal Implications

Take time to reflect on the implications of James 2:1–13 for your own life today. Make notes below on the personal implications for your walk with the Lord of (1) the *Gospel Glimpses*, (2) the *Whole-Bible Connections*, (3) the *Theological Soundings*, and (4) this passage as a whole.

1. Gospel Glimpses

---

2. Whole-Bible Connections

---

3. Theological Soundings

_____

_____

_____

_____

_____

_____

_____

4. James 2:1–13

_____

_____

_____

_____

_____

_____

_____

> ## As You Finish This Unit . . .

Take a moment now to ask for the Lord's blessing and help as you engage in this study of James. And take a moment also to look back through this unit of study, to reflect on a few key things that the Lord may be teaching you—and perhaps to highlight or underline these to review again in the future.

Definitions

[1] **Salvation** – Deliverance from the eternal consequences of sin. Jesus' death and resurrection purchased eternal salvation for believers (Rom. 1:16).

[2] **Judgment** – Any assessment of something or someone, especially moral assessment. The Bible also speaks of a final day of judgment when Christ returns, when all those who have refused to repent will be judged and condemned (Rev. 20:11–15).

WEEK 6: FAITH WITHOUT WORKS IS DEAD

James 2:14–26

To this point in his letter, James has been making the case that once the new birth has happened to a person, it should result in a life of *doing* God's word. In the first part of chapter 2, he began working that principle out in one specific example—his readers' wrong practice of showing partiality to the rich and powerful. Now, in 2:14–26, he returns to the principle itself, arguing theologically and biblically for its truth. Faith, James argues, always results in a life of obedience and good works.[1] And a "faith" that does not do so is not saving faith at all; it is, rather, dead faith.

The Big Picture

Faith, if it does not produce works, is not really faith at all; it is dead faith that does not save.

> ## Reflection and Discussion

Read through the complete passage for this study, James 2:14–26. Then review the shorter passages below and write your own notes on the following questions. (For further background, see the *ESV Study Bible*, pages 2394–2395, also available online at esv.org.)

1. Faith without Works (2:14–17)

Verses 14 and 17 best encapsulate James's main point in this section of his letter. What is his main point? When he says that faith needs to "have works" in order to be saving, does he mean that works need to be *added to* faith, or that works should *naturally grow from* faith?

Look at the three times James uses the word "faith" in these four verses. Each time, he is talking about something that is actually *less than*—and therefore *not at all*—genuine, saving faith. What textual clues do you see that would signal James's understanding that this is not genuine faith? (Hint: The first time he uses the word, he says "if someone *says* he has faith," not "if someone *has* faith." What similar clues show up in the second and third uses of the word?)

James's understanding of the relationship between faith and works seems to be something like the planting of a seed. If a seed (faith) is truly alive, it will produce a plant (works). If it doesn't produce a plant, however, it does not do any good to grab a plant and stick it into the soil above the seed. That doesn't make the seed any more alive; it is still dead! In the same way, James is not saying that faith is dead until works are added to it. On the contrary, faith is only alive if it naturally produces good works—in the same way as a seed is only alive if it naturally produces a plant. Adding good works to faith no more makes faith alive than cramming a plant on top of a seed makes the seed alive. Understanding that, explain verse 17 in your own words.

----

2. Response of a Critic (2:18–20)

In verse 18 James begins a brief conversation with an imaginary opponent. "You have faith and I have works," the opponent says. In other words, some people have faith and others have works, but both aren't necessary. James counters by asserting that, no, faith and works are vitally connected. "Show me your faith apart from your works!" he challenges. "You can't! Because the way you know faith is alive—the way you show it to be real—is by the works that come from it." How does James's comment about demons' "faith" in verse 19 help to establish his point?

What's the difference between merely correct theology and genuine, living faith?

----

3. Examples of Abraham and Rahab (2:21–26)

After taunting his imaginary opponent by asking if he wants to be shown that faith which doesn't issue in works is useless, James uses the examples of Abraham and Rahab to illustrate his point. In verse 21, what does the phrase mean which says that Abraham's "faith was completed by his works?" (Hint: a seed comes to maturity in a plant.) Is he saying that faith is alive but deficient until we add works to it? (Hint: Is a seed alive but deficient until we add a plant to it?)

The word "fulfilled" in verse 23 has the sense of "reaching its intended goal." James is saying that Abraham's belief in God (and his resulting justification) reached their intended goal and came to maturity in his act of obedience to God when he offered Isaac on the altar. Is this understanding (that faith grows to maturity in a life of obedience) different from what Paul teaches elsewhere? Can you think of any verses from Paul's letters that teach the same thing?

Verse 24 has caused significant confusion among Christians, because it seems to formally contradict Paul's teaching that we *are* in fact justified by faith alone. Justification, however, has two different meanings in Scripture. On the one hand is Paul's somewhat technical use of the word to mean "a judicial declaration, an acquittal and declaration that a person is to be regarded as righteous." And Paul says that this justification happens through faith alone, on the basis of Christ's righteousness alone. On the other hand, however, is an older and more common meaning of justification as "a public presentation of a person as being righteous" (e.g., Matt. 11:19; Luke 7:29; Rom. 3:4). Think of it as the difference between a wedding minister's *pronouncement* that a couple are man and wife and his *public presentation* of them to the congregation as people who are acting in a way that is consonant with the pronouncement he has just made. Keeping in mind that James probably wrote his letter several years before Paul wrote his epistles, which of those two senses of "justify" do you think James is using here?

Is there any formal contradiction between the following two statements?

A. "A person is judicially declared righteous through faith alone, on the basis of Christ's righteousness alone."
B. "A person is publicly presented as righteous—that is, publicly vindicated as being righteous—not on the basis of faith alone, but on the basis of a life of obedience which shows that person's professed faith to be real."

Explain how both A and B can be true at the same time. Are James and Paul in contradiction to each other?

In verses 25–26 James uses another example to teach this same point—that faith, if it is real, will result in a life of obedience. Is he saying that Rahab was *judicially declared righteous* on the basis of her obedience, or that she was *publicly shown to be righteous* by her obedience?

Read through the following three sections on *Gospel Glimpses*, *Whole-Bible Connections*, and *Theological Soundings*. Then take time to reflect on the *Personal Implications* these sections may have for your walk with the Lord.

Gospel Glimpses

JUSTIFICATION BY FAITH. James does not at all denigrate the place of faith in salvation. On the contrary, he affirms it over and over again. In 2:14, for example, he does not at all question the truth that it is faith which saves; he simply takes aim at a *certain kind* of "faith"—dead faith—and says that it will not save. In 2:23 as well, James affirms that Abraham was judicially acquitted through his mere belief in God. He simply goes on to state that Abraham's justifying faith came to fulfillment—reached its maturity—in a life of obedience. Therefore, James is not in contradiction to Paul at any point. When we realize that the word "justification" is used with two different senses—*judicial acquittal* and *public presentation*—we see that James and Paul are fully agreed.

THE NATURE OF FAITH. James uses the word "faith" without ever really defining what he means by it. Nevertheless, we can see hints of his understanding of it in this section. Abraham had faith, and that is described in 2:23 as "believing God." In other words, faith is trusting in God to keep his promises. This side of Jesus' incarnation, faith finds its rightful object in him. We trust Christ to represent us, to live and die in our place, and thereby to save us from our sin.

Whole-Bible Connections

ABRAHAM'S FAITH TESTED. In Genesis 22, God tells Abraham to take Isaac, his son (and the fulfillment of God's promise to make him a great nation!) and sacrifice him on a high mountain. Abraham, because he trusts God, obeys, though God stays his hand at the last moment. James draws on that moment of testing to show that Abraham's faith in God was not a dead faith. On the contrary, it was a living faith. He genuinely trusted God, and that trust naturally gave rise to a life of obedience.

RAHAB'S FAITH SHOWN BY HER OBEDIENCE. In Joshua 2:8–11, Rahab tells the Israelite spies that she has heard the stories of how their God rescued them from Egypt, dried up the Red Sea before them, and defeated their enemies. Moreover, she believed that those stories were true, trusting in the God about whom they were told. Her belief, however, did not just stop at an intellectual assent. It worked itself out in action—in the protection of the messengers. The story of Rahab thus makes James's point quite powerfully. Faith is not just mental assent, nor is it just an intellectual profession. Faith, if it is alive, will result in works. And faith by itself, if it does not result in works, is dead—that is, it is no real faith at all.

Theological Soundings

GOD'S JUDICIAL ACQUITTAL OF US IS THROUGH FAITH ALONE. Both James and Paul are agreed on this. Paul is very clear on this point in Romans 3 and throughout Galatians, and James too is clear in multiple places (1:18; 2:14–17; 2:23) that it is faith which becomes the occasion and the instrument of God's judicial declaration of his people as righteous. We believe in Christ, and we are declared righteous on the basis of his life, death, and resurrection in our place.

LIVING FAITH WILL EXPRESS ITSELF IN OBEDIENCE. This has been James's point throughout his book, but Paul is entirely agreed. In Romans 12:1–2, for example, he writes: "I appeal to you, therefore, brothers, by the mercies of God, to present your bodies as a living sacrifice, holy and acceptable to God, which is your spiritual worship. Do not be conformed to this world, but be transformed by the renewal of your mind, that by testing you may discern what is the will of God, what is good and acceptable and perfect." And in Colossians 3:1–3, 12–13 he says, "If then you have been raised with Christ, seek the things that are above, where Christ is, seated at the right hand of God. Set your minds on things that are above, not on things that are on earth. For you have died, and your life is hidden with Christ in God . . . Put on then, as God's chosen ones, holy and beloved, compassionate hearts, kindness, humility, meekness, and patience, bearing with one another and, if one has a complaint against another, forgiving each other; as the Lord has forgiven you, so you also must forgive."

DEAD FAITH DOES NOT SAVE. Again, James has been very clear about this point, and Paul agrees. In Ephesians 4:17 and 5:3–5, Paul says to professing Christians, "Now this I say and testify in the Lord, that you must no longer walk as the Gentiles do, in the futility of their minds. . . . But sexual immorality and all impurity or covetousness must not even be named among you, as is proper among saints. Let there be no filthiness nor foolish talk nor crude joking, which are out of place, but instead let there be thanksgiving. For you may be sure of this, that everyone who is sexually immoral or impure, or who is covetous (that is, an idolater), has no inheritance in the kingdom of Christ and God." Simply professing faith in Christ is not enough, Paul says. Your profession of faith must result in a life of holy, authentic obedience.

Personal Implications

Take time to reflect on the implications of James 2:14–26 for your own life today. Make notes below on the personal implications for your walk with the Lord of (1) the *Gospel Glimpses*, (2) the *Whole-Bible Connections*, (3) the *Theological Soundings*, and (4) this passage as a whole.

1. Gospel Glimpses

2. Whole-Bible Connections

3. Theological Soundings

4. James 2:14–26

As You Finish This Unit . . .

Take a moment now to ask for the Lord's blessing and help as you engage in this study of James. And take a moment also to look back through this unit of study, to reflect on a few key things that the Lord may be teaching you—and perhaps to highlight or underline these to review again in the future.

Definitions

[1] **Works** – Actions and attitudes, either good or bad. True faith in Christ will inevitably produce good works that are pleasing to God. Good works, however, can never be the basis or means of salvation, which is by grace alone through faith alone.

WEEK 7: TAMING THE TONGUE

James 3:1–18

In the last passage, James laid out the theological and biblical case for his main point—that a living, genuine faith will lead to a life of obedience. For the rest of the book now, James will consider several areas of his readers' lives where obedience is necessary. The issues he addresses seem to have been particular struggles for his readers. In 3:1–18 James considers how his readers are using their tongues to tear one another down with strife and backbiting. Instead of doing that, he says, they ought to be people of meekness and wisdom. That is what Christian obedience would demand.

The Big Picture

Christians should be careful not to let their tongues cause strife and quarrels, but rather use them in wisdom to make peace in the church.

> **Reflection and Discussion**

Read through the complete passage for this study, James 3:1–18. Then review the shorter passages below and write your own notes on the following questions. (For further background, see the *ESV Study Bible*, pages 2395–2396, also available online at esv.org.)

1. The Trouble with the Tongue (3:1–12)

The main topic of this passage is the evil of the tongue. Why do you think James starts the section with the exhortation that "not many of you should become teachers"? (Hint: if a lot of sinful people are aspiring to the same position in the church, what can be the result?)

Read verse 2. What does James think would be the *hardest* area of life in which to avoid stumbling?

In verses 3–5 James uses three examples to explain the power of the tongue, despite its physical smallness. What are the three examples? Explain James's point in your own words.

Verses 6–12 contain some of the most blistering language in the New Testament, which James directs against the tongue. What phrases does James use in verse 6 to describe the tongue's evil? Write out each phrase in the verse, and explain what each means. (Use the note on 3:5–5 in the *ESV Study Bible* for help.)

What is the contrast James draws in verses 7–8? What is James communicating about the tongue?

In verses 9–12 James points out a fundamental tension in our use of the tongue. The tongue does two things at once—blessing and cursing! What three examples does James use in verses 11 and 12 to show the absurdity and sinfulness of using the same tongue to bless God and curse people?

Do you think the tongue deserves everything James is ascribing to it here? Does it really cause that much trouble? Why do you give that answer?

2. The Solution: Wisdom from Above (3:13–18)

If the tongue is so dangerous, what should we do about it? James has already said in 1:26 that obedience to the word of God requires us to bridle the tongue. His point seems to be similar here. Instead of being driven by the evil of the tongue, we should be marked by "the meekness of wisdom." Can you find places in 3:1–12 that show how the tongue can be marked by pride instead of meekness[1]?

Why would somebody *boast* about having bitter jealousy and selfish ambition in their heart? Why would they confuse those things with "the wisdom that comes down from above" (v. 15)? (Hint: if your heart is filled with bitter jealousy, you probably don't recognize it as such; you probably call it "a desire for fairness" and insist on the wisdom of your position!)

Explain how a church full of jealousy and selfish ambition can collapse into disorder and vileness (v. 16).

Read verses 17–18 and notice all the words James uses to describe a person marked by wisdom from above. How are those things opposed to bitter jealousy and selfish ambition?

Read through the following three sections on *Gospel Glimpses, Whole-Bible Connections,* and *Theological Soundings.* Then take time to reflect on the *Personal Implications* these sections may have for your walk with the Lord.

▶ Gospel Glimpses

WE BLESS OUR LORD AND FATHER. Overarching all of James's ethical exhortations is the reality that we as Christians are in relationship with God, our Lord and Father. That is the fundamental reality of a Christian's life, and it shapes everything he or she does, says, and thinks.

FULL OF MERCY. The wisdom from above, James says, is, among other things, "full of mercy" (James 3:17). The wise man or woman is not reluctant to extend mercy to another, but eager. For those who know the wisdom from above are the very ones who have been granted mercy in Christ. God, in Jesus, was "full of mercy" toward us. We have the glad privilege of extending that mercy accordingly to others.

▶ Whole-Bible Connections

THE TONGUE AND WISDOM. How we use our tongue is an important theme in Old Testament Wisdom Literature, and James draws from that wealth of knowledge in this section. In Psalm 120:2–4, the psalmist prays, "Deliver me, O LORD, from lying lips, from a deceitful tongue. What shall be given to you, and what more shall be done to you, you deceitful tongue? A warrior's sharp arrows, with glowing coals of the broom tree!" (see also Prov. 16:27). Our tendency to use our tongue for evil is one of the most important pieces of evidence the Bible uses to show us our sinfulness and our need for a Savior. In his Sermon on the Mount Jesus says, "But I say to you that everyone who is angry with his brother will be liable to judgment; whoever insults his brother will be liable to the council; and whoever says, 'You fool!' will be liable to the hell of fire" (Matt. 5:22). In his famous collection of Old Testament verses showing our sinfulness, Paul also uses the tongue as evidence of our sinfulness: "Their throat is an open grave; they use their tongues to deceive." "The venom of asps is under their lips." "Their mouth is full of curses and bitterness" (Rom. 3:13–14).

THE MEEKNESS OF WISDOM. Meekness and humility are terms frequently used to describe a person of wisdom (Prov. 18:12; 22:4). That is because wisdom begins with the fear of the Lord (Prov. 1:7), which requires a willingness to submit to instruction and teaching and to obey the Lord's word. Pride does not desire to submit to any such thing, and therefore it prevents one from becoming wise. All of that is a distinctively biblical teaching. The Greeks did not consider meekness to be a virtue at all. It was Jesus, drawing on Old Testament teaching, who made meekness a cardinal virtue of a Christian (Matt. 5:5; 11:29).

Theological Soundings

THE IMAGE OF GOD. The Bible teaches that all of us are created in God's image and likeness. In Genesis 1:26 God says that he is going to make man "in our image, after our likeness." Some Christians have argued, on the basis of Genesis 5:3, that it was only Adam who was made in God's likeness, and all his descendants are made in *Adam's* likeness, not God's. This understanding is proved to be mistaken by James 3:9. All people are made in the likeness of God, although none naturally behave in a godlike way. One implication of this creational godlikeness is that humanity has been given the capacity for language. Let us use the tongue, therefore, in a way that honors others, who are equally created in God's image.

Personal Implications

Take time to reflect on the implications of James 3:1–18 for your own life today. Make notes below on the personal implications for your walk with the Lord of (1) the *Gospel Glimpses*, (2) the *Whole-Bible Connections*, (3) the *Theological Soundings*, and (4) this passage as a whole.

1. Gospel Glimpses

---

2. Whole-Bible Connections

3. Theological Soundings

4. James 3:1–18

As You Finish This Unit . . .

Take a moment now to ask for the Lord's blessing and help as you engage in this study of James. And take a moment also to look back through this unit of study, to reflect on a few key things that the Lord may be teaching you—and perhaps to highlight or underline these to review again in the future.

Definitions

[1] **Meekness** – Humble assurance under all circumstances, founded on a deep trust in God's will and providence (Ps. 37:11). Such trust results in a peaceful and gentle disposition even in the face of persecution or difficulty. It frees a person from the temptations of self-reliance and pride.

WEEK 8: THE CAUSE OF QUARRELS

James 4:1–12

The Place of the Passage

In chapter 3 James began dealing with the problem of quarreling and back-biting within the church. The immediate issue seems to have been people competing with one another for position within the church (3:1), and they were using their tongues to tear one another down. Having spoken about the tongue's evil and the power of wisdom to counteract it, James turns in chapter 4 to consider the quarrels themselves. In a brilliant explanation of human nature, fallen as it is, he shows that quarrels are the result of unfulfilled, prideful desires warring within us, and he then exhorts his readers to repent of their pride.

The Big Picture

Fights and quarrels are caused when we desire something and cannot get it. The remedy for that kind of pride is repentance and submission to God.

> ## Reflection and Discussion

Read through the complete passage for this study, James 4:1–12. Then review the shorter passages below and write your own notes on the following questions. (For further background, see the *ESV Study Bible*, pages 2396–2397, also available online at esv.org.)

1. The Cause of Quarrels (4:1–5)

In verses 1–3 James gives us a profound analysis of human conflict. People have wondered for centuries what causes conflict, and they have given multiple answers to the question: differing philosophies, inaccurate assumptions, differing expectations, differences in culture, differing conflict resolution strategies. James, however, cuts right to the root. He gives an answer that is so self-evidently true that it now seems inescapably obvious to us, something that, once said, can never be denied. What is James's answer? "What causes quarrels and what causes fights among you?"

In verse 2, is James accusing members of the church of actually, physically killing each other? (Hint: read Matthew 5:21–22 before you answer.)

Ponder verse 3. Is every desire a good desire? How do you tell the difference between a good desire and a bad one?

In verses 4–5 James makes the point that you cannot be driven by ungodly desires and expect to be in friendship with God. Where else in the Bible is this truth taught?

There is no specific verse of Scripture that says precisely, word for word, what James says in verse 5. Is James misquoting Scripture? Look at the *ESV Study Bible* notes on James 4:5 and James 3:14. Which theme of Scripture's teaching is James probably referencing in this verse?

---

2. The Nature of Repentance (4:6–10)

In verse 6, what does James say is the antidote to the prideful desires that cause quarrels?

In verses 7–10 James exhorts believers to do seven things in order to counter-act pride in their lives. List those seven exhortations, and explain what James means by each of them.

---

3. Who Are You to Judge? (4:11–12)

In verses 11–12 James returns to the main theme of these last few verses—the way some in the Christian community were speaking evil of one another out of jealousy and a selfish ambition for status in the church. "Do not speak evil against one another, brothers." But read the rest of verse 11. What is the reason James gives for not speaking evil against each other?

To what specific commandment does James point in 2:8 as summing up or encapsulating the heart of King Jesus' royal law? How is it a violation of that commandment to speak evil against a brother?

When you know what the law says and deliberately decide not to obey it, but rather to violate it, what are you implicitly saying about that law? (Hint: that it is unworthy of your obedience, etc.) What right do you have to say such things about God's law? Now, having answered those questions, put James's point in verses 11 and 12 in your own words.

To paraphrase James's last question in verse 12, what right do you have to violate the heart of the royal law by judging your brother instead of loving him?

Read through the following three sections on *Gospel Glimpses, Whole-Bible Connections,* and *Theological Soundings.* Then take time to reflect on the *Personal Implications* these sections may have for your walk with the Lord.

Gospel Glimpses

FRIENDSHIP WITH THE WORLD IS ENMITY WITH GOD. James teaches here that becoming a Christian involves a radical break with sin. A person cannot continue to coddle and entertain his sin and still claim to be a Christian. This is simply a matter of repentance—of turning away from sin and toward God. The power for doing this is the gospel message itself, through which we have been turned from enemies to friends of God. This truth, made real to us by the Holy Spirit, frees us to accept becoming an enemy of the world in various ways. Through the gospel, we have the one friendship that matters.

ONE LAWGIVER AND JUDGE, WHO IS ABLE TO SAVE AND TO DESTROY. James puts the fundamental choice presented in the gospel in stark terms here. All human beings are sinful and therefore liable to condemnation and eternal punishment—that is, to destruction according to God's exacting justice. In his grace, however, God has determined to save all those who turn from sin and trust his Son, Jesus, to save them from their sin.

Whole-Bible Connections

A JEALOUS GOD. From the very beginning of his dealings with the nation of Israel, God made it clear that he would not tolerate his people worshiping gods other than himself. So in the first of the Ten Commandments he says, "I am the LORD your God, who brought you out of the land of Egypt, out of the house of slavery. You shall have no other gods before me" (Ex. 20:2–3). For this reason, God repeatedly described himself as "jealous," even saying in Exodus 34:14 that his very *name* is "Jealous." Ezekiel and Amos, too, draw out the idea of God's jealousy, comparing him to a husband whose wife has been unfaithful. God is passionate about his people's faithfulness to him. As James seems to be saying, he has given us life, and he expects our single-minded worship in return.

THE LAW AND DIVINE JUDGMENT. Unlike the other nations of the world, the nation of Israel did not develop its own law. Rather, Israel's Lawgiver was God himself. In the book of Exodus, God calls Moses to the top of Mount Sinai and gives him the law according to which Israel is to live. Not only so, but it is God and God alone who will judge the world. As he promises in Joel 3:12, "Let the nations stir themselves up and come up to the Valley of Jehoshaphat; for there I will sit to judge all the surrounding nations." It is striking that in the New Testament, both of these roles—Lawgiver and Judge—are assumed by the Son of God. In Matthew 5, Jesus claims for himself the role of Lawgiver, and therefore the right to say what the law really means (Matt. 5:17–20). Not only so, but it is Jesus who assumes the role of Judge as well: "When the Son of Man comes in his glory, and all the angels with him, then he will sit on his glorious throne. Before him will be gathered all the nations, and he will separate people one from another as a shepherd separates the sheep from the goats" (Matt. 25:31–32).

Theological Soundings

YOUR PASSIONS ARE AT WAR WITHIN YOU. Christians are not exempt from the battle against sin. Even after we experience the new birth and the Lord gives us a new heart, we still battle against our old sinful nature. Paul writes about this struggle in Galatians 5:16–17: "But I say, walk by the Spirit, and you will not gratify the desires of the flesh. For the desires of the flesh are against the Spirit, and the desires of the Spirit are against the flesh, for these are opposed to each other, to keep you from doing the things you want to do." As Christians, we are forgiven of our sin and set free from its dominion, but we will need to continue to struggle against it until we are finally with Jesus (1 John 1:10).

RESIST THE DEVIL. James understands that the devil, or Satan,[1] is a real being, not just a symbol of the world's evil. This is a reality taught throughout the Bible. Jesus often interacted with malign, personal spiritual beings, and so did the apostles, as the book of Acts shows. Part of our calling as Christians is to resist the devil and his plots in our lives.

Personal Implications

Take time to reflect on the implications of James 4:1–12 for your own life today. Make notes below on the personal implications for your walk with the Lord of (1) the *Gospel Glimpses*, (2) the *Whole-Bible Connections*, (3) the *Theological Soundings*, and (4) this passage as a whole.

1. Gospel Glimpses

2. Whole-Bible Connections

3. Theological Soundings

4. James 4:1–12

As You Finish This Unit . . .

Take a moment now to ask for the Lord's blessing and help as you engage in this study of James. And take a moment also to look back through this unit of study, to reflect on a few key things that the Lord may be teaching you—and perhaps to highlight or underline these to review again in the future.

Definitions

[1] **Satan** – A spiritual being whose name means "accuser." As the leader of all the demonic forces, he opposes God's rule and seeks to harm God's people and accuse them of wrongdoing. His power, however, is confined to the bounds that God has set for him, and one day he will be destroyed along with all his demons (Matt. 25:41; Rev. 20:10).

WEEK 9: SINS OF THE WEALTHY

James 4:13–5:6

The Place of the Passage

In this passage, James continues to unfold his main point that new life in Christ should result in a life of obedience to God's Word. Here he addresses particularly the sins of the wealthy. First he addresses the sin of pride in those who would forget that their lives are completely in the hand of the Lord. Then he turns to warn of the coming judgment against those who would use their wealth and power to oppress God's people. This is some of the most strident language in the book, and it underlines the sin and folly of human pride—especially when our pride sets us in opposition to God and his people.

The Big Picture

None of us finally controls the circumstances and outcomes of our lives; God does. Therefore we should not be prideful, but rather humble ourselves before God.

▶ Reflection and Discussion

Read through the complete passage for this study, James 4:13–5:6. Then review the shorter passages below and write your own notes on the following questions. (For further background, see the *ESV Study Bible*, pages 2397–2398, also available online at esv.org.)

1. Boasting about Tomorrow (4:13–17)

Verses 13–17 are a straightforward assault on human pride and presumptuousness. Describe the kind of person to whom this section seems to be addressed. What kind of enterprise do these people seem to be engaged in? Do they seem to be poor or fairly affluent?

Do you think the people addressed in these verses are professing Christians? What clues in the text lead you to that conclusion? (Hint: look carefully at v. 15.)

What mistake are these businesspeople making in their assumptions (vv. 13–14)? What sins underlie these mistaken assumptions?

What does James say ought to be a Christian's frame of mind when thinking about the future? Is James saying that planning or investing for the future is wrong? If not, what then is he saying *is* wrong?

Do you think you should actually *say* the phrase "if the Lord wills" when you talk about the future? Even if it's not necessary to say it every time, how can you work to cultivate that kind of dependence on God in your own life and thinking?

Essentially, James is here taking aim at the human tendency to think we are in control. What kinds of bad effects does a godless sense of self-sovereignty have in our lives?

----

2. Warning to the Rich (5:1–6)

If the paragraph in 4:13–17 is addressed to Christians, to whom is the paragraph in 5:1–6 addressed? What clues in the text help you describe these people?

This paragraph contains blistering language against wealthy landowners who are oppressing God's people. As in so much of his letter, James is here resonating deeply with the teaching of the Old Testament. Can you think of some places in the Old Testament that address similar warnings to powerful oppressors?

In what ways were these rich landowners oppressing the church? Give specific examples from the text.

James says that instead of being proud and reveling in their riches and power, they should be doing what? Why?

In what areas of your life do you have a certain degree of power? How do you use it? For example, how do you treat your employees? The family who rents your property? The person who cleans your office building or school? The person who makes your food at a restaurant? Do you treat them as means to the end of your own self-indulgence, or do you treat them as people whom God has put in your life for you to love and care for?

How can you rightly take comfort—as believers do throughout the Bible—at the thought of God's final judgment of evil, and yet not violate Romans 12:19?

Read through the following three sections on *Gospel Glimpses*, *Whole-Bible Connections*, and *Theological Soundings*. Then take time to reflect on the *Personal Implications* these sections may have for your walk with the Lord.

Gospel Glimpses

A DIFFERENCE BETWEEN CHRISTIANS AND NON-CHRISTIANS. One interesting pattern in James's letter is how he treats Christians and non-Christians differently. In these paragraphs, for example, notice the way James addresses his audience in 4:13–17. In verse 15, for example, he corrects their thinking in an effort to make them more Christian in the way they think and talk about their lives. That is not true of his audience in 5:1–6. In that passage, there is no exhortation to the oppressors to change. Rather, there is simply the promise of judgment—a judgment that for believers has already fallen on Christ at the cross.

FAITH IN JESUS OR FAITH IN RICHES. In 5:1–6 James takes powerful oppressors to task for reveling in and relying on their power and material goods. His point is that those things in which they have put their faith—riches, garments, gold and silver, power—will be of no value at all in the last day. The only reality that is worthy to be relied on is Jesus.

A DAY OF JUDGMENT COMING. James has no doubt at all that a day of final judgment is coming, when God will set everything right. He warns the rich of this in 5:1–6, and he'll turn in 5:7 to tell believers to hope in the coming of that day. The great message of the gospel is that although we all deserve to be condemned on that day, through Jesus God has "brought us forth" and given

71

us new life (1:18). He has made us "a kind of firstfruits of his creatures." The day of judgment therefore holds no terror for us as Christians, because our faith is in Jesus and not in ourselves, our possessions, or our power.

Whole-Bible Connections

WISDOM ABOUT TOMORROW. As he does so often in his book, James draws in this passage on Old Testament wisdom. The Israelites knew that their God was sovereign over the events of their lives, and so they exhorted one another not to be prideful about what they would or would not do tomorrow. Proverbs 27:1, for example, says, "Do not boast about tomorrow, for you do not know what a day may bring."

THE BREVITY OF LIFE. In 4:14 James reminds his readers of how brief and fragile their lives are, echoing what he had already said in 1:11. This is a common theme in both the Old Testament and the New Testament. Psalm 39:5, for example, compares human life to a breath. (See also Job 7:6–7; Ps. 89:47; and other places.) Peter also points his readers to the brevity of life: "All flesh is like grass, and all its glory like the flower of grass" (1 Pet. 1:24).

Theological Soundings

GOD'S METICULOUS SOVEREIGNTY. James's exhortation that Christians should say "if the Lord wills" comes from his understanding that God is sovereign[1] over all the details of our lives. We see this throughout the pages of the Bible. Even Joseph, when he reflected on the evil that his brothers had done to him in selling him into slavery in Egypt, said, "You meant evil against me, but God meant it for good" (Gen. 50:20). And in Acts 4:27–28, the believers affirm, in prayer to God, that, when Pilate and Herod and the leaders of the Israelites put Jesus to death, they were doing "whatever your hand and your plan had predestined to take place." God is sovereign over all the details of our lives, and that is a source of great comfort to us as Christians.

THE DAY OF JUDGMENT. The language James uses in 5:1–6 points forward to a final day of judgment when God will fully and finally set everything right. At the close of history, Jesus the King will return and judge the living and the dead according to their deeds. Sin will be condemned, injustice set right, and oppression ended. For those who are outside of Christ, it is a day to be dreaded. For those whose faith is in Christ, however, it is a day to which we look forward with both joy and deep sobriety.

> ## Personal Implications

Take time to reflect on the implications of James 4:13–5:6 for your own life today. Make notes below on the personal implications for your walk with the Lord of (1) the *Gospel Glimpses*, (2) the *Whole-Bible Connections*, (3) the *Theological Soundings*, and (4) this passage as a whole.

1. Gospel Glimpses

2. Whole-Bible Connections

3. Theological Soundings

4. James 4:13–5:6

> ### As You Finish This Unit . . .

Take a moment now to ask for the Lord's blessing and help as you engage in this study of James. And take a moment also to look back through this unit of study, to reflect on a few key things that the Lord may be teaching you—and perhaps to highlight or underline these to review again in the future.

Definitions

[1] **Sovereignty** – Supreme and independent power and authority. Sovereignty over all things is a distinctive attribute of God (1 Tim. 6:15–16). He directs all things to carry out his purposes (Rom. 8:28–29).

WEEK 10: PATIENCE IN SUFFERING

James 5:7–12

The Place of the Passage

Having warned the rich and powerful oppressors of God's people about the coming judgment, James turns now to encourage the church with the same reality. One day, Jesus Christ will come again to rescue his people from those who oppress and persecute them. He will put an end to injustice and evil. In light of that reality, God's people should live and wait patiently, as a farmer waits patiently for his crops to grow from the earth. That patience is warranted precisely because God has shown himself faithful. He will, without fail, keep his promises, just as he always has.

The Big Picture

God's people should wait patiently for God to keep his promise to judge the wicked and rescue his people from oppression.

> ## Reflection and Discussion

Read through the complete passage for this study, James 5:7–12. Then review the shorter passages below and write your own notes on the following questions. (For further background, see the *ESV Study Bible*, pages 2398–2399, also available online at esv.org.)

1. Be Patient in Suffering (5:7–9)

What is the main exhortation that James gives to his readers in this paragraph? Why do they need that exhortation?

What illustration does James use to show his readers the meaning of patience? How would that illustration help them understand what he is exhorting them to do?

What does the phrase "establish your hearts" mean, practically speaking? How does the reality of Jesus' return help you to do that?

Are there circumstances in your life under which you need to be patient? What are they? What truths help you to be patient under those trials?

What function is verse 9 playing? Why does James warn about grumbling? How could a heart that is not "established" lead a person to grumble? What lies at the root of most grumbling, and how could having an established heart cut that root?

2. Examples of Patience (5:10–12)

Why does James point to examples of patience? How do examples from the Bible help us to see what God wants from us, and the importance of those things?

James says that "the prophets" are "an example of suffering and patience." About whom do you think James is talking there? What examples from the Old Testament can you think of in which someone endured suffering with patience?

In verse 11 James mentions two things that should give believers comfort and encouragement to stand fast in their trials. What are those two things?

How does being reminded of the steadfastness of Job encourage you to stand fast as well? How does being reminded of the "purpose of the Lord," that is, "how the Lord is compassionate and merciful," encourage you to stand fast?

What is James doing with verse 12? How does ungodly oath-making (like the grumbling in verse 9) reveal a heart that is not steadfast and established? How does an unestablished heart lead to ungodly oath-making?

Do you think there is any connection or resonance between 5:12 and 4:13–15? If so, what is the connection?

Read through the following three sections on *Gospel Glimpses, Whole-Bible Connections,* and *Theological Soundings.* Then take time to reflect on the *Personal Implications* these sections may have for your walk with the Lord.

Gospel Glimpses

LOOKING FORWARD TO THE COMING OF THE LORD. It's interesting that James treats the coming of the Lord very differently in this passage than he did in 5:1–6. There, the day of the Lord was a fearful thing, bringing only destruction and condemnation. Here, it is actually something to be longed for; it is to bring comfort and solidity to a Christian's life. The difference, of course, is between James's two audiences. In 5:1–6, he is talking to people who are not Christians, who have not submitted to the Lord Jesus in faith and repentance. In 5:7–12, on the other hand, the focus is on those who have repented and believed in Jesus. It is a stark—and eternal—difference that James sketches. Believers joyfully await the coming of the Lord Jesus, by whose work all our sins are forgiven and heaven awaits, won for us through the victory of another.

THE COMPASSION AND MERCY OF THE LORD. James reminds us again in 5:11 how the Lord is compassionate and merciful. Those truths lie at the very heart of the good news of Christianity. It is God's love for sinners—his mercy and compassion—which led him not simply to leave them in their sin, but rather to act in Jesus Christ so that they might be saved. As Paul said, "God shows his love for us in that while we were still sinners, Christ died for us" (Rom. 5:8).

Whole-Bible Connections

THE STEADFASTNESS OF JOB. Job is a paradigmatic example in the Old Testament of patience in suffering. Tested by Satan through the death of his family and the loss of everything he owned, Job prayed to God and questioned him, but he never cursed God or turned his back on him. He remained faithful and was commended in the end. Job's faithful patience is held out for us here as an example we are to follow as we face our own trials and temptations.

CHRIST'S COMING. "You also, be patient. Establish your hearts, for the coming of the Lord is at hand" (James 5:8). In Eden, the Lord dwelt and walked with Adam and Eve. The fall fractured this fellowship and God withdrew. From that point on he was accessible only through special visions or, mainly, at a later stage, in the tabernacle and the temple. In Christ, however, the Lord came into this now darkened world. In the middle of history, God began decisively to restore the fellowship that was lost in Eden. And at the end of history, Christ will come a second time, as the Lord returns one final time to restore the cosmos to its Edenic state. James calls believers to be patient in light of that great hope.

Theological Soundings

THE COMING OF THE LORD IS AT HAND. The Bible teaches that the return of the Lord Jesus to bring his people home and consummate his kingdom will be "soon" (Rev. 22:20). Of course, what that means finally is up to God, for whom a day is like a thousand years, and a thousand years like a day (2 Pet. 3:8). God is not bound by time as we are. He is eternal, and so we would be wrong to accuse him of being slow. After all, what is two thousand years—or a hundred thousand!—to the eternal God? The point is that we do not know when Christ will return, and so we ought to be ready for that glorious moment all the time. The Christian life is to be one of readiness, not laxity.

DIVINE SOVEREIGNTY. Remarkably, James speaks of the "purpose of the Lord," not "the purpose of Satan" in describing Job's nightmare experiences (James 5:11). Though Satan was working most immediately and directly in Job's affliction, all was done under the sovereign and good hand of God—a God who "is compassionate and merciful" (5:11). Job himself indicates that he understood this (Job 1:21; 2:10). Even the hellish experiences of life are under the providential, all-ruling hand of our heavenly Father.

Personal Implications

Take time to reflect on the implications of James 5:7–12 for your own life today. Make notes below on the personal implications for your walk with the Lord of (1) the *Gospel Glimpses*, (2) the *Whole-Bible Connections*, (3) the *Theological Soundings*, and (4) this passage as a whole.

1. Gospel Glimpses

2. Whole-Bible Connections

3. Theological Soundings

4. James 5:7–12

> ## ▶ As You Finish This Unit . . .

Take a moment now to ask for the Lord's blessing and help as you engage in this study of James. And take a moment also to look back through this unit of study, to reflect on a few key things that the Lord may be teaching you—and perhaps to highlight or underline these to review again in the future.

WEEK 11: THE PRAYER OF FAITH

James 5:13–20

The Place of the Passage

One of the main points James has been making throughout his letter has been that Christians should not just profess faith in God, but they should live lives that reflect the reality of their profession. In other words, they should live in a way that underscores their declaration that God really exists. James 4:13–17, as well as chapter 5 to this point, have been emphasizing this. In 5:13–20 now, James continues to make that point. One of the main ways we live in light of God's reality is to pray to him. He hears prayer, and he answers it. Prayer is powerful.

The Big Picture

Prayer is powerful because God hears and answers it.

Reflection and Discussion

Read through the complete passage for this study, James 5:13–20. Then write your own notes on the following questions. (For further background, see the *ESV Study Bible*, page 2399, also available online at esv.org.)

Without yet getting hung up on some of the more difficult details in this passage, what do you think is the main point James is trying to make to his readers? How is he trying to encourage them?

How does the illustration about Elijah in verses 17–18 underline James's main point? What specifically is James trying to get across when he says that Elijah was "a man with a nature like ours," and then goes on to point out the powerful effects of his prayer? What is he aiming to tell us about prayers and the God who hears them?

Verses 14–16 have been the occasion for much debate and disagreement among Christians. There are several things at issue. First of all, do you think James is there talking about a *physically* sick person, or a person who is *spiritually* sick or weak? (Hint: remember that James draws heavily on Jesus, and in Jesus' teaching, the words used here for "sick" are always used of physical sickness!)

What do you think the oil signifies? Some have argued that it is an example of the sacrament of "extreme unction," in which a person is anointed with oil just before death to absolve them of sin. Do you see anything in the text that would suggest that? (Hint: no!) Others have suggested that the use of the oil is medicinal. That's possible, but do you see anything in the text that would lead you to think that the point is something else—that it is not primarily just medicinal? After all, why would medicine need to be applied by the elders in particular? In your answer consider the purpose of oil in the anointing[1] of a king or priest. Read Exodus 30:30. What does it mean to "consecrate" someone?

In verse 16, James connects sickness and sin. Can each and every sickness be traced back to a particular sin? (Hint: read John 9:2–3.) Can sickness *sometimes* be traced back to a particular sin? (Hint: read John 5:14 and 1 Cor. 11:29–30.) Given that, what do you think James is saying in verse 16?

What does James mean by saying that "the prayer of faith will save the one who is sick?" What is the prayer of faith? Does he mean that if you simply have enough faith, God will always heal—and that if God doesn't heal, it's your fault for not having enough faith? Read 2 Corinthians 12:7–9. Was Paul's prayer there not very faithful? Read Philippians 2:25–27. Were Paul's prayers for Epaphroditus not faithful enough until Epaphroditus was almost dead? Read 2 Timothy 4:20. Did Paul not pray hard enough and faithfully enough before he left Miletus?

Many people believe that James is talking about a special gift of faith—that is, a gift of extraordinary certainty that God gives to a person when he has already determined to heal someone. First Corinthians 12:9 may be talking about a gift of faith like that. How does that understanding of a gift of faith according to God's will differ from an understanding that would say James is commanding us to work up enough faith within ourselves so that people will be healed through our praying?

Another possibility is that James is simply picking up again on the teaching of Jesus, which he does often. In that case, he would simply be teaching about the power of praying with faith, just as Jesus often did. Read Matthew 21:21–22. Those verses sound just as absolute as James's saying that "the prayer of faith *will* save the one who is sick," but they also assume the theological truth that God is sovereign—that is, *he* determines how he will answer our prayers. In other words, you will get what you ask for when you pray in faith *if what you ask for is in line with God's will.* That is a truth stated explicitly in 1 John 5:14–15, but it underlies all the Bible's teaching about prayer. If that's the case, then what is James's meaning when he says, "And the prayer of faith will save the one who is sick?"

Once we understand all the details, James's point comes through loud and clear: prayer is powerful, and God *wants* to answer prayer! Do you pray with the understanding that God desires to answer our prayers, or do you pray with the expectation that he won't answer them?

Verses 19–20 form a conclusion to the whole book of James. What does James exhort us as Christians to do for each other? What is the benefit of our caring for one another in that way?

Read through the following three sections on *Gospel Glimpses*, *Whole-Bible Connections*, and *Theological Soundings*. Then take time to reflect on the *Personal Implications* these sections may have for your walk with the Lord.

Gospel Glimpses

FORGIVENESS. "And if he has committed sins, he will be forgiven" (James 5:15). For those who have grown up in the church, such a promise may seem unremarkable. But consider what is being said by James here. Sins are not forgiven through some act of self-atoning. Sinners do not need to feel sorry intensely enough or berate themselves long enough. This goes against our natural intuitions. James says that all that needs to be done is open, honest, penitent confession. That is how sins are forgiven. In the world of the gospel, we are freed from the masks we all tend to wear. We can be honest about who and what we truly are. For in Christ, we are fully and freely accepted.

BRINGING BACK A SINNER. The gospel is about saving sinners from their sin and the death that results from it. In the last sentence of his letter, James reminds us of that fundamental fact. Sin leads to death, and therefore a sinner who is brought to repentance is one who has saved his soul from death. James has been clear throughout the book: this is no small matter. It is a matter of life and death, judgment and salvation. Praise be to God, who through Jesus Christ makes a way for sinners to be brought back. The work of Christ is fully able to "cover a multitude of sins" (5:20).

Whole-Bible Connections

PRAYER. "Let him pray" (James 5:13). Prayer lies at the heart of this closing passage of James and is a recurrent theme throughout the entire Bible. Adam and Eve walked with God in Eden and therefore had full access to God. Yet after the fall this fellowship broke, and Genesis tells of the time when "people began to call upon the name of the LORD," not having previously done so (Gen. 4:26). The Old Testament goes on to describe the complex system of sacrifices and offerings that were God-given ways for prayerful sinners to be in contact with God once more. When Christ came, he too taught his disciples to pray (Matt. 6:5–13). And at the end of history, when Christ returns, once more full fellowship with God will be restored (Rev. 21:1–4). Our faith will become sight (2 Cor. 5:7).

ELIJAH. The story of Elijah's prayer and the resulting drought is told in 1 Kings 17–18. The drought was a divine punishment on King Ahab and the people of Israel for their disobedience and idolatry. Elijah and Moses appeared with Jesus at the Transfiguration (Mark 9:2–13). Elijah represented the Prophets and Moses represented the Law, both of which Jesus brought to fulfillment. Indeed, Jesus is ultimately the prophet like Elijah who was to come and turn the hearts of God's people back to God himself (Mal. 4:5–6).

Theological Soundings

THE POWER OF PRAYER. The Bible is consistent in its teaching that prayer is powerful and effective. Ours is a God who hears the prayers of his people and who delights to answer them.

Personal Implications

Take time to reflect on the implications of James 5:13–20 for your own life today. Make notes below on the personal implications for your walk with the Lord of (1) the *Gospel Glimpses*, (2) the *Whole-Bible Connections*, (3) the *Theological Soundings*, and (4) this passage as a whole.

1. Gospel Glimpses

2. Whole-Bible Connections

3. Theological Soundings

4. James 5:13–20

As You Finish This Unit . . .

Take a moment now to ask for the Lord's blessing and help as you engage in this study of James. And take a moment also to look back through this unit of study, to reflect on a few key things that the Lord may be teaching you—and perhaps to highlight or underline these to review again in the future.

Definitions

[1] **Anoint** – In Scripture, to pour oil (usually olive oil) on someone or something to set the person or thing apart for a special purpose. Anointing was performed for the high priest, for tabernacle vessels, for kings, and for prophets. The Hebrew word Messiah and its Greek equivalent Christ both mean "Anointed One."

WEEK 12: SUMMARY AND CONCLUSION

▲

As we come to the end of our study of the book of James, it will be good for us to consider the big picture of the book as a whole. Then, we will take a final look at Gospel Glimpses, Whole-Bible Connections, and Theological Soundings in James, all with a view toward understanding James's letter in its entirety and hearing his heart and exhortation to us as Christians.

The Big Picture of James

James is sometimes accused of having written a book that really has no internal organization—no structure and no driving point, but is rather a hodgepodge of unrelated issues thrown together haphazardly. Studying the book carefully, however, it's easy to see how false that charge is. James does have a driving point, and it is this: now that God has given us new life (1:18), we should live in such a way that this new life is reflected in our actions. We are to be doers of the word and not just hearers of it. Our faith is to be a living faith, which produces good works, not dead faith, which is really no faith at all.

James drives this point home throughout his book, holding up issue after issue for consideration in light of that main point. In chapter 1, he talks about how

91

a follower of Jesus will handle trials and temptations. In chapter 2, he tells followers of Jesus how they should act in the presence of powerful people and weak people. In chapter 3, he tells them how a Christian should control his or her tongue, and in chapter 4 he discusses how Christians should handle conflict with other people. Finally, in chapter 5, he reminds us to live as Christians in the eager anticipation and certainty of Christ's imminent return.

Read through the following three sections on *Gospel Glimpses, Whole-Bible Connections*, and *Theological Soundings*. Then take time to reflect on the *Personal Implications* these sections may have for your walk with the Lord.

Gospel Glimpses

James has often been accused of not having a deep understanding of the gospel. It is sometimes argued that his is a sub-biblical understanding of Christianity, that it is a purely ethical or even moralistic conception of what it means to be a Christian. That could not be further from the truth!

Throughout our study of James, we have seen how deeply he understands the truth of the gospel. He affirms strongly that being a Christian is about being born again, not just doing good things (1:18). He agrees with the rest of the New Testament that a living faith saves (2:14), and that it was in fact faith that was credited to Abraham as righteousness (2:23). He looks forward to the second coming of Jesus Christ (5:7–8).

The desire of James's heart is simply to help believers think more clearly about how to *live* in light of all those things. If he doesn't give as full an explanation of the gospel as some other books of the New Testament, it is not because he doesn't believe it or understand it. It is because he understands it and believes it *deeply* and is focusing on the life of obedience that should flow from it.

Have you ever wondered why James doesn't contain as full and detailed an explanation of the gospel as other books of the New Testament? In your own words, describe James's focus in this book and how the gospel is crucial to that focus.

Has your understanding of the gospel changed at all during the course of this Bible study?

How has James helped you to understand the gospel better than you did before you started this study?

Are there any particular passages in James that have brought the gospel home to you in a fresh way?

Whole-Bible Connections

James has been called the Proverbs of the New Testament, and it's easy to see why. As a Jewish man who came to faith in Jesus, James is steeped in the imagery and wisdom of the Old Testament. He also obviously learned deeply from the teaching of Jesus, his brother and his Savior. Therefore, his letter is filled with themes from and allusions to both the Old Testament and the teaching of the Lord Jesus. His warnings to the unbelieving rich and powerful about the coming judgment are deeply reminiscent of both the Old Testament and Jesus. His teaching about wisdom draws heavily on Old Testament Wisdom Literature, as do his exhortations about the tongue. And his teaching about prayer and oaths, among other things, show how much he learned from Jesus.

James is also quick to use Old Testament examples to make his points. He uses Abraham and Rahab in chapter 2, the prophets and Job in 5:10–11, and Elijah in 5:17. James's mind is filled with the Word of God, and when he needs an illustration for his points, his mind naturally goes to the Scriptures to fill that need.

How has your understanding of the place of James in the sweep of the Bible's story been deepened through your study of this letter?

What are some connections between James and the Old Testament that you had not noticed before? What are some connections between James and the teaching of Jesus that you had not noticed before?

Has your understanding of the unity of the Bible been clarified through studying James? How so?

Theological Soundings

James contributes a great deal to Christian theology, especially regarding how to practically work out the teachings of Jesus. Doctrines that are reinforced and clarified in James include regeneration, the doctrine of the Word of God, wisdom, divine sovereignty, prayer, and the relationship between justification, faith, and works.

Where has your theology been molded or corrected as you have studied James?

_____
_____
_____
_____
_____

How might our understanding of God and the gospel of Jesus Christ be impoverished if we did not have James's letter?

_____
_____
_____
_____
_____

How does James contribute to our understanding of Jesus?

_____
_____
_____
_____
_____

How does he contribute to our understanding of the gospel?

_____
_____
_____
_____
_____

How does he contribute to our understanding of what it means to be a Christian?

_____
_____
_____
_____
_____

Personal Implications

As you consider the book of James as a whole, what implications do you see for your own life? Consider especially James's exhortation that we are to be doers of the word, and not hearers only. More than anything else, this is the organizing center of James's letter. What are the ramifications for your own life of James's exhortation there?

As You Finish Studying James . . .

We rejoice with you as you finish studying the book of James! May this study become part of your Christian walk of faith, day by day and week by week throughout all your life. Now we would greatly encourage you to continue to study the Word of God on a week-by-week basis. To continue your study of the Bible, we would encourage you to consider other books in the *Knowing the Bible* series, and to visit www.knowingthebibleseries.org.

Lastly, take a moment again to look back through this book of James, which you have studied during these recent weeks. Review again the notes that you have written, and the things that you have highlighted or underlined. Reflect again on the key themes that the Lord has been teaching you about himself and about his Word. May these things become a treasure for you throughout your life—which we pray will be true for you, in the name of the Father, and the Son, and the Holy Spirit. Amen.